4-2011

OIL SPILL DISASTER

Scholastic Inc.
New York • Toronto • London • Auckland
Sydney • Mexico City • New Delhi • Hong Kong

Acknowledgments

The authors would like to thank Roger Anderson, Nancy Kinner, Jon Kolak, Tom MacKenzie, and Barbara Schroeder for sharing their voices and expertise. Not only did these scientists provide insight into the causes and effects of the Deepwater Horizon disaster, they also helped verify the content of this book.

Written by Mona Chiang, Cody Crane, Karina Hamalainen, and Lynda Jones

Designed by Mojo Media
Joe Funk, Jason Hinman

Photo Research: Steven Diamond, Deborah Kurosz, Jeff Paul, and Veroniqua Quinteros
Production Editor: Elizabeth Krych
Editorial Assistant: Rebecca Cox
Intern: Greta Friar

Photographs © 2010: cover main: US Coast Guard/Richard Brahm; cover left inset: Reuters/Hans Deryk; cover center left inset: Reuters/Sean Gardner; cover center right inset: NEWSCOM/Carolyn Cole; cover right inset: Reuters/BP handout/Ho New; back cover main: AP Images/Jae C. Hong; back cover left inset: AP Images/Charlie Riedel; back cover center left inset: AP Images/Charlie Neibergall; back cover center right inset: AP Images/Patrick Semansky; back cover right inset: AP Images/Alex Brandon; page 1: AP Images/Charlie Riedel; page 2, 3: US Coast Guard; page 4-5 background: Corbis Images/Julie Dermansky; page 6-7 background: AP Images/Dave Martin; page 6 top: NEWSCOM; page 6 bottom: Getty Images/BP; page 7 top: Getty Images/Natalie B. Forbes/National Geographic; page 7 center: Library of Congress; page 8 top: National Geographic Image Collection/Sarah Leen; page 8 bottom background: iStockphoto/P_Wei; page 9 top: Courtesy of U.S. Geological Survey/Jon Kolak; page 10 background: ShutterStock, Inc./Marafona; page 10 top right: ShutterStock, Inc./Daryl Marquardt; page 10 top left: ShutterStock, Inc./joyfull; page 10 center right: ShutterStock, Inc./GWImages; page 10 bottom left: ShutterStock, Inc./Khafizov Ivan Harisovich; page 10 bottom right: ShutterStock, Inc./Krivosheev Vitaly; page 11 background: ShutterStock, Inc./traff; page 11 bottom: ShutterStock, Inc./Paul B. Moore; page 12 inset: AP Images/Hasan Jamali; page 12-13 background: AP Images/Transocean; page 14-15, 18-19: AP Images/Gerald Herbert; page 20-21 background: AP Images/Dave Martin; page 20 inset: AP Images/Alex Brandon; page 21 top inset: UNH Photographic Services/Nancy Kinner; page 21 bottom inset: US Coast Guard/Chief Petty Officer John Kepsimelis; page 22-23 background: ShutterStock, Inc./Mario7; page 22 top right: Getty Images/Sue Flood; page 22 top left: ShutterStock, Inc./Steve Noakes; page 22 bottom left: NOAA/Brandi Noble Collection; page 22 bottom right: Getty Images/Thomas Haider; page 23 top: ShutterStock, Inc./Phillip W. Kirkland; page 23 right center: ShutterStock/Mikhail Matsonashvili; page 23 left center: Courtesy of NOAA; page 24 right: Courtesy of US Coast Guard/Adam C. Baylor; page 25 top: AP Images/Charlie Riedel; page 25 bottom left: AP Images/Charlie Riedel; page 25 bottom center left: AP Images/Janet McConnaughey; page 25 bottom center: AP Images/Charlie Riedel; page 25 bottom center right: Corbis Images/Julie Dermansky; page 25 bottom right: AP Images/Rick Silva; page 26 left: AP Images/US Coast Guard; page 26 bottom: Reuters/BP; page 27: Courtesy of Roger Anderson; page 28-29 background: Courtesy of Roger Anderson; page 29 bottom: Getty Images/Win McNamee; page 28 top: Getty Images/Derick E. Hingle; page 28 bottom: Matteroftrust.org; page 29 top: Courtesy of Vidnya Iyer; page 30-31 background: ShutterStock, Inc./Mikhail Dudarev; page 31 wind, solar, hydro icons: ShutterStock, Inc./SimonasP; page 31 geothermal icon: ShutterStock, Inc./huihuixp1; page 31 biomass icon: ShutterStock, Inc./Marco Rullkoetter; page 32: AP Images/Dave Martin

Diagram illustrations on pages 8, 10, 17, and 26 by Chris Borseau
Map and charts on pages 4, 7, 9, 11, and 30 by Mojo Media Art Bank

Table of Contents

Louisiana

Mississippi   Alabama

Georgia

Florida

Oil Slick ——————   —— Site of Explosion

Gulf of Mexico

This map shows the site of the Deepwater Horizon
explosion and the area of the oil slick on June 14, 2010.

"This oil spill is the worst environmental disaster America has ever faced...

The Gulf of Mexico is an American treasure. In this body of water swims a great variety of marine life, including fish and shrimp. Along its coasts are nesting grounds for seabirds and turtles. And deep beneath the seabed is a rich reserve of oil and natural gas.

Many people who live in the five U.S. states that border the Gulf of Mexico—Texas, Louisiana, Mississippi, Alabama, and Florida—depend on the Gulf for jobs and survival. The fishing industry draws as much as 1.3 billion pounds of fish and shellfish from the Gulf each year. And along the coastline, approximately 4,000 offshore rigs drill for valuable oil and gas.

But on April 20, 2010, disaster struck the region. An oil rig located 41 miles (66 kilometers) off the coast of Louisiana exploded. The disaster killed 11 people who worked onboard.

The rig, named Deepwater Horizon, was drilling for oil about a mile below sea level. A series of glitches triggered the explosion. The damaged well caused millions of gallons of oil and gas to gush upward. A massive oil slick spread across the Gulf of Mexico. The thick and gooey oil smothered seabirds and fish. Dead marine turtles washed up on beaches. But the greatest damage may be invisible for now. Marine biologists warn that the plumes of oil from the seabed could change the Gulf's ecosystem forever.

Why did Deepwater Horizon explode? What did experts do to contain the oil spill? How does the spill affect lives? What is oil and why do we need it in the first place?

... and unlike an earthquake or a hurricane, it's not a single event that does its damage in a matter of minutes or days. The millions of gallons of oil that have spilled into the Gulf of Mexico are more like an epidemic, one that we will be fighting for months and even years." — President Barack Obama, June 15, 2010

Catastrophic Records

The disaster in the Gulf stunned the nation. But it was not the first oil spill to have originated in the United States. An oil spill can happen in many places. It can happen at the well, as in the case of Deepwater Horizon. It can also happen when oil is being transported by oil tankers or through pipelines. Depending on the location and size of the accident, spills can cause a lot of damage. Here are some of the worst oil spills in U.S. history.

Deepwater Horizon Spill

Date: April 20, 2010 • Location: Gulf of Mexico

In just the first week after the rig's explosion, the broken well spewed more than 250,000 barrels of oil into the ocean. The U.S. government declared the incident a national disaster. Because the oil spill was widespread, it polluted and damaged vast areas. The oil's toxins also affected large populations of wildlife.

RECORD: Worst Offshore Oil Spill in U.S. History

Trans-Alaska Pipeline Spill

Date: March, 2006 • Location: Prudhoe Bay, Alaska

The Trans-Alaska Pipeline was built in the 1970s to efficiently transport oil from the Prudhoe Bay oil fields in the north to the port of Valdez in the south. Over time, pipes like these can rust and holes can form. That's what happened in 2006 to a section owned by BP that connects its oil field to the Trans-Alaska pipeline.

A dime-sized hole in the north end of the pipeline leaked as much as 6,400 barrels of oil. The oil had been leaking for at least five days before BP oil workers noticed it. The spilled oil covered two acres of land. After the accident, the BP portion of the pipeline was shut down for more than a year while repairs were made to 16 miles (26 kilometers) of the pipe system.

RECORD: Longest Undetected Leak in the U.S.

Exxon Valdez Spill

Date: March 23, 1989 • Location: The Alaska Coast

The tanker *Exxon Valdez* sailed from the Trans-Alaska Pipeline terminal, carrying a cargo of approximately 1.3 million barrels. Three hours into its journey, the tanker ran into Bligh Island Reef in Prince William Sound, Alaska.

A gash in the side of the tanker poured more than 250,000 barrels of oil into the sound. That's enough to fill 17 Olympic-sized swimming pools! The oil slick killed as many as 2,800 sea otters, 300 harbor seals, 22 killer whales, 250 bald eagles, 250,000 seabirds, and billions of salmon and herring eggs. Today—more than 20 years after the spill—most of the oil has been cleaned up, but there are still places where oil can be found.

RECORD: Worst Tanker Spill in the U.S.

Lakeview Gusher

Date: March 15, 1910 • Location: Kern County, California

A grocery salesman named Julius Fried purchased a patch of land, hoping to strike it rich with oil. Fried drilled for months without success. But on the day the drill hit 2,200 feet (670 meters) below the surface, the well erupted. It gushed uncontrollably for 18 months, spewing 9 million barrels of oil. Workers used barricades to try to hold back the flood. About 5 million barrels of oil were captured and sold.

RECORD: Worst Oil Spill on U.S. Soil

Top Five Worst Oil Spills in the World

Where will the Deepwater Horizon spill rank in history?

Name	Location	Year	Cause	Amount (in barrels)
1. Lakeview Gusher	California, USA	1910	Blowout	9,000,000
2. Gulf War oil spill	Persian Gulf	1991	Intentional	6,000,000 to 11,000,000
3. Ixtoc I oil rig	Gulf of Mexico	1979	Blowout	3,300,000
4. *Atlantic Empress/Aegean Captain*	Trinidad and Tobago	1979	Ship collision	2,143,000
5. Fergana Valley oil spill	Uzbekistan	1992	Blowout	2,000,000

Who Needs Oil?

Without oil, most people's lives would come to a complete stop. Oil is important because it provides the world with much of its energy needs. Fuels made from oil power cars, airplanes, and other vehicles. Oil products heat people's homes. But you may be surprised to learn what things you use every day that are made from oil.

Just look at the items around you. There is a good chance that many of them contain key ingredients that are made from oil. Plastic is one of the most common of these. You'll also likely find oil-derived ingredients in sneakers, makeup, candles, clothing, crayons, furniture, gum, ink, laundry detergent, medicines, paint, toothpaste, and toys. The list is nearly endless.

Oily Household

This photo shows a family surrounded by all their belongings that contain an ingredient made from oil.

Where Oil Comes From

Oil is made from plants and animals that lived millions of years ago. Here's how these organisms turned into oil.

   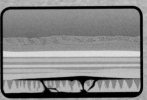

1. Microscopic plants and animals, such as plankton, float in the sea. When they die, their remains drift slowly to the seafloor.

2. Over time, the decaying, or rotting, organisms collect in a thick sludge. Layers of mud and sand slowly cover the remains. Eventually, the layers build up and bury the remains below the seafloor.

3. Deep underground, there is a lot of pressure on the remains. At the same time, the remains get cooked by the high temperatures from Earth's interior. Over millions of years, these combined forces change the remains into oil and change the mud and sand layers into rock.

4. The oil slowly seeps upward through tiny holes and cracks found in surrounding rocks. The oil becomes trapped when it reaches a rock layer that doesn't have these openings. The oil pools to form a reservoir.

Energy Expert

Name: Jon Kolak • Job: Associate coordinator for the Energy Resource Program at the U.S. Geological Survey (USGS)

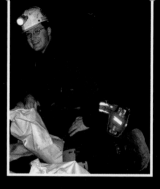

What do you do?

I am a scientist at the USGS, a government agency that studies the science of Earth. I help research energy resources, such as oil and coal, found in the United States and the world.

How dependent on oil are humans?

The world uses more than 30 billion barrels of oil a year. Oil is a nonrenewable resource. Once we use it up, the fuel is gone for good. That's because it takes millions of years for it to form. But technological, environmental, social, and economic factors could change how much we rely on oil.

How might we reduce the amount of oil we use?

More and more people are starting to use renewable energy, such as solar and wind power. These types of energy naturally replenish much more quickly than nonrenewable resources like oil. People are also more aware of how much oil they use. For example, when shopping for cars, more people now search for fuel-efficient models. People are also reusing things made from oil, like plastic goods.

Top 10 Oil-Consuming Nations

This chart shows how many barrels a day each nation consumes.

Rank	Country	Consumption
1.	United States	19,498,000
2.	China	7,831,000
3.	Japan	4,785,000
4.	India	2,962,000
5.	Russia	2,916,000
6.	Germany	2,569,000
7.	Brazil	2,485,000
8.	Saudi Arabia	2,376,000
9.	Canada	2,261,000
10.	South Korea	2,175,000

Source: Energy Information Administration

Using oil is nothing new. Humans have been using this natural resource for more than 5,000 years. Ancient cultures set fire to oil for light. They painted oil on boats and houses to keep the structures waterproof. They also used oil as glue, to make bricks, and even to preserve bodies as mummies.

Humans' dependence on oil continues today. Oil is now the world's top energy source. The United States alone uses more than 19 million barrels of oil in a day — that's more than any other country in the world.

Black Gold

Oil is valuable because there is a high demand for its many uses. That's why oil is nicknamed "black gold."

Oil forms deep under the earth, and oil companies compete to dig for this precious substance. When oil is drawn from the ground, it is a dark and sticky liquid called crude oil. This raw material can't be used right away. It needs to be processed in refineries.

These factories are a complex system of pipes, tanks, and towers. Some refineries operate around the clock to separate oil into different oil products.

How Crude Oil Turns Into Oil Products

① Crude oil is heated to approximately 750°F (400°C), turning it into gas.

② The oil vapor flows into a tower, which is divided into horizontal sections.

③ As gas moves up the tower, it cools. The gas condenses, turning back into a liquid. Some substances in the vapor condense at higher temperatures. Some substances condense at lower temperatures. As a result, the oil ends up divided into several fractions, or parts. Oil from separate fractions is turned into different products.

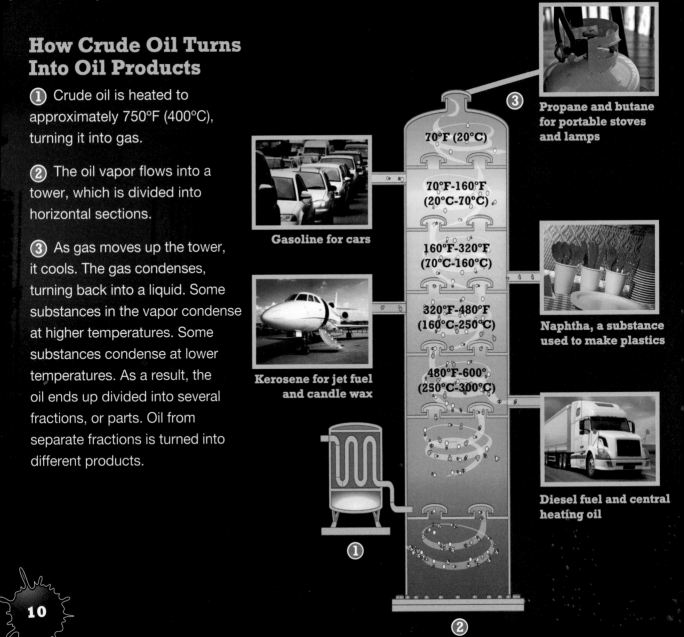

③ **Propane and butane for portable stoves and lamps**

70°F (20°C)

70°F-160°F (20°C-70°C)

Gasoline for cars

160°F-320°F (70°C-160°C)

320°F-480°F (160°C-250°C)

Naphtha, a substance used to make plastics

Kerosene for jet fuel and candle wax

480°F-600° (250°C-300°C)

Diesel fuel and central heating oil

① ② ③

The World's Oil

Oil can be found all over Earth, but some areas have more oil than others. Most of the world's crude oil, a dark and sticky liquid, is found in the Middle East. This region is home to more than half of Earth's oil reserves. Within this region, Saudi Arabia harbors the world's largest oil reserves of all.

The United States produces some oil, too. It can produce approximately 5,310,000 barrels a day, an amount far short of meeting the nation's demands. More than one-fourth of the crude oil produced in the United States comes from offshore drilling in the Gulf of Mexico.

U.S. Crude Oil Production

This diagram shows where and how many barrels of crude oil are produced in the country each day.

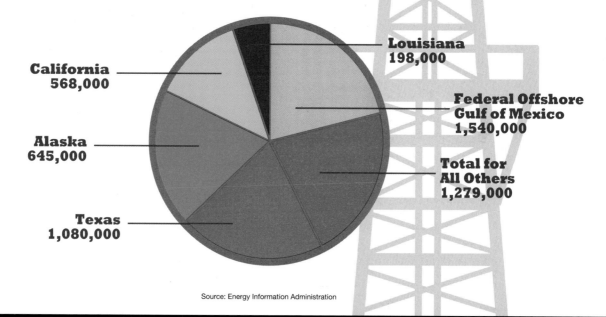

California
568,000

Louisiana
198,000

Federal Offshore
Gulf of Mexico
1,540,000

Alaska
645,000

Total for
All Others
1,279,000

Texas
1,080,000

Source: Energy Information Administration

Quest for Oil

Since oil is buried deep underground, how do oil companies zero in on the black gold? They hire geologists to study rock formations and look for where oil may pool underground. When an oil reserve is found, companies set up drilling rigs that can bore through rock. The rigs dig deep down, often several miles under the earth, to reach the oil reserve. Then the rigs pump the gooey crude oil to the surface.

ing Deep in the Gulf

2009, BP filed a plan with the federal government's Minerals Management Sevice
Gulf of Mexico. The well was planned for an oil reservoir called the Macondo
the Louisiana coast. Geologists calculated that the reservoir could contain more
on barrels of oil. The plan was reviewed and approved.

in February 2010, a massive floating oil platform, Deepwater Horizon, began to drill
loor. The platform was the size of two football fields, and would drill at a depth of
ely 5,000 feet (1,500 meters).

Life on an Offshore Rig

Oil platforms are usually far from shore,
so the workers stay onboard for weeks at
a time. These platforms come equipped
with sleeping areas and cafeterias. To keep
the crew entertained, many platforms are
outfitted with facilities such as gyms and
movie theaters. Hundreds of people work
on an offshore platform. Jobs range from
drilling for oil to cooking food for the crew.
The oil-drilling crew is made up of workers
called roustabouts and roughnecks.

Roustabouts help maintain the rigs. They do
everything from unloading heavy supplies
to cleaning up messy areas. A roustabout
can be promoted to become a roughneck.
These workers are in charge of drilling.
They also guide pipes into the oil well.

Deepwater Horizon's job was to explore for oil and gas. Once they were found, the well would be capped off with cement. Unfortunately, no one was prepared for what happened next.

Disaster Strikes

On Tuesday, April 20, 2010, workers tried to place a temporary cement seal on the well.

But something went wrong and the seal broke.

At approximately 9:45 p.m., a geyser of natural gas and oil erupted up the well. When the flammable gas hit the platform, a spark from somewhere on the rig caused the gas to catch fire and explode.

No one knows what ignited the gas. But anything from a small spark created by a tool scraping the platform's deck to someone welding in the onboard machine shop could have done it. The flames shot a hundred feet into the air. There were 126 people working on the Deepwater Horizon at the time. Eleven crewmembers died. The rest barely escaped by lifeboats.

The Cause of the Blowout

The contents of a well are like bubbles trapped in a very large soda bottle. Oil and natural gas are lighter than rock and water and so they naturally push upward. This push creates pressure.

The Deepwater Horizon's drill created enough counterpressure to keep the oil and natural gas in place. But the Macondo reservoir was larger than anticipated and so was the amount of pressure inside the well. The cement seal wasn't strong enough to handle the pressure. This miscalculation led to the blowout.

Oil Spill

Emergency responders battled the flames that erupted on Deepwater Horizon, but they failed. The entire rig sank to the seafloor in two days. But an even bigger disaster brewed deep below sea level.

The explosion caused the riser pipe that connected the oil well to the platform to bend and break. Three different safeguards designed to prevent leaks all failed. Oil and gas gushed through the broken pipe and surged into the deep ocean waters. No one is certain how much oil actually spewed out. Experts estimate the volume could be more than 35,000 barrels each day. Over the following months, the U.S. Coast Guard, various government agencies, and officials from BP dashed to find ways to stop the leak and protect the Gulf Coast from the spreading oil slick.

This is the actual size of the drill pipe—the inner, hollow part of the riser pipe. Much of the oil leaked from this 6.625-inch (16.827-centimeter) pipe.

The riser pipe is 21 inches (53.34 centimeters) in diameter.

How the Safeguards Failed

Here are three places where things went wrong:

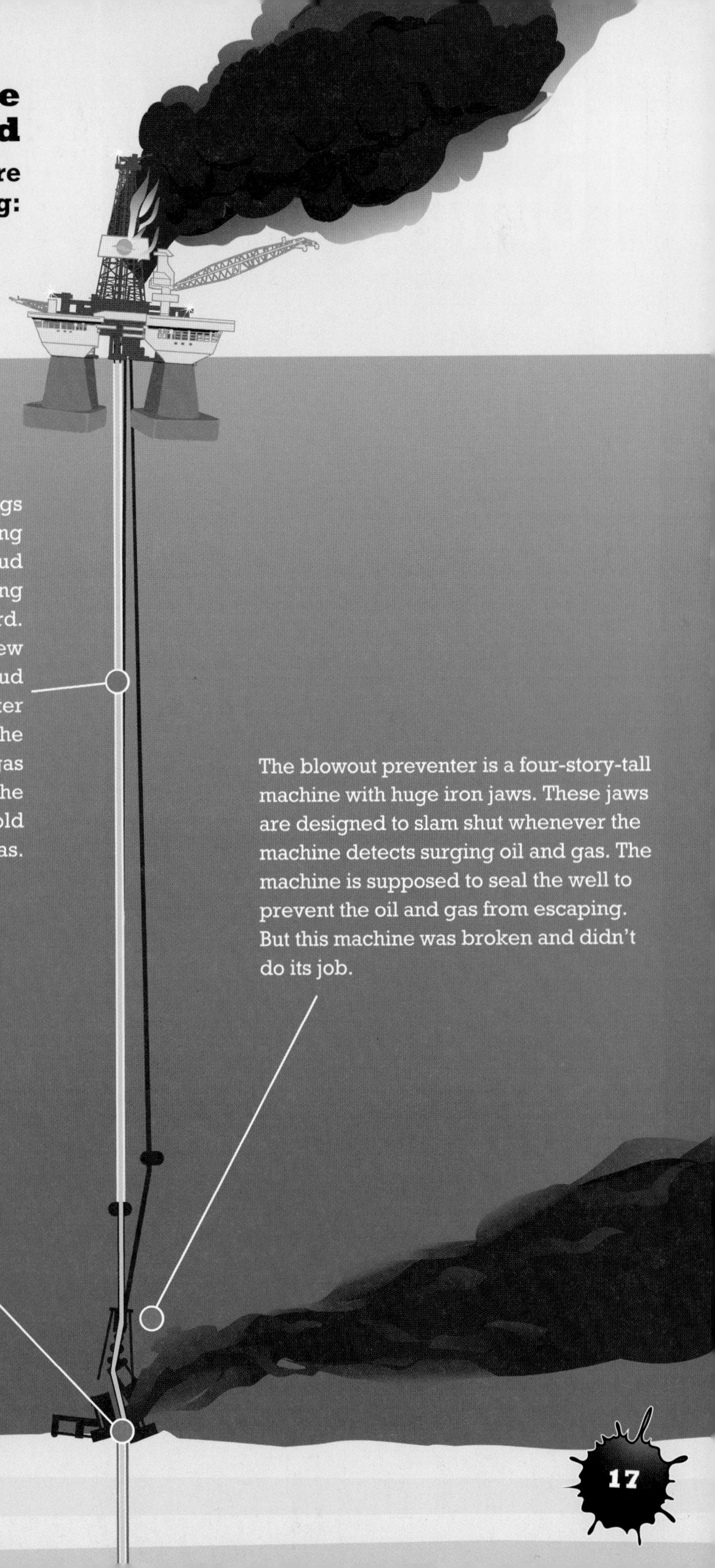

During the drilling process, oil rigs continually pump thick and heavy drilling mud up and down the riser pipe. This mud puts pressure on the well, preventing the oil and gas from gushing upward. To prepare for the arrival of a new production platform, BP removed the mud and replaced it with much lighter seawater. The company thought that the cement plug would hold the oil and gas down. When the cement plug failed, the water inside the drill pipe could not hold back the erupting oil and gas.

The blowout preventer is a four-story-tall machine with huge iron jaws. These jaws are designed to slam shut whenever the machine detects surging oil and gas. The machine is supposed to seal the well to prevent the oil and gas from escaping. But this machine was broken and didn't do its job.

A cement plug at the bottom of the well is supposed to keep oil and gas from pushing its way to the surface. But the cement failed.

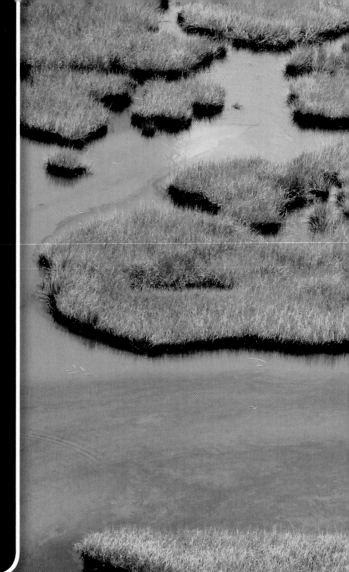

Environmental Damage

Some experts estimate the amount of oil spilled by Deepwater Horizon could easily blanket an area over 2,500 square miles (6,400 square kilometers). That's a bit larger than the state of Delaware.

Oil spills are tricky to clean up because they do not stay put. Ocean currents and weather conditions cause the oil to travel far and away.

To tackle the moving target, BP met with the Coast Guard, the National Oceanic and Atmospheric Administration, and others to figure out what areas of the U.S coastline were at the greatest risk and would need the most urgent cleanup. Some of the biggest danger zones are wetlands and coastal waters.

"On a normal day, there would be dozens of shrimp boats and fishing boats out there with big catches, but instead we had vacuum barge operations working to suction up the heavy oil that is now coating this important wildlife habitat. This spill is having a direct impact on our way of life."

— Louisiana governor Bobby Jindal, June 15, 2010

Priority Zone: Wetlands

Where the Mississippi River empties into the Gulf of Mexico are numerous wetlands, such as marshes and swamps. These areas are filled with a large variety of plant and animal species. But that's not all. The wetlands are also important barriers against hurricanes.

The grasses in the wetlands help trap the fine silt and soil that flow from the Mississippi River to the Gulf. This trapped material helps build a barrier along the coast. This "front line" can act as a shield, protecting inland areas from getting flooded by storms that blow in from the sea. If oil smothers and kills the grasses in the wetlands, this natural defense erodes.

Priority Zone: Coastal Waters

The coastal waters and the wetlands serve as the foundation of the Gulf's seafood trade. A lot of the fishing industry's key organisms like crab, shrimp, oysters, and fish breed and live here. The Gulf of Mexico provides up to 67 percent of the U.S. oyster supply. Gulf fisheries also provide the country with three-fourths of its shrimp harvest.

In the summer of 2010, a large area off the Louisiana coast—about one-third of the Gulf of Mexico—was declared off-limits to fishing, shrimping, and harvesting oysters. The government wanted to make sure that oil-tainted seafood did not wind up on consumers' plates. Because of this, many people in the seafood industry lost their jobs.

Operation: Spill Control

To prevent oil from spreading toward the coast, emergency response workers deployed special equipment to clean up the oil slick.

Booms

One way to manage an oil slick is to rope it off. Workers used booms, which are temporary floating barriers, to surround the oil-tainted waters. Then they tugged on the booms to corral the oil. Over five and a half million feet of boom were used during the Gulf spill.

Skimmers (Pictured at right)

Workers also used skimmers to remove oil from the water's surface. These devices come in many different shapes and sizes, but they all work the same way. Skimmers suck in tainted water and "vacuum" the oil that is floating on top. The cleaned water is then pumped back out to sea. Some skimmers used during the Gulf oil spill collected as much as 36,500 barrels of oil each day.

Health Risks

Oil contains toxic chemicals. One, called benzene, is a known cancer-causing agent. When oil is burned, it emits poisonous gases such as carbon monoxide. Exposure can harm the respiratory system and irritate the eyes and skin.

Cleanup Expert

Name: Nancy Kinner • Job: Director of the Coastal Response Research Center, University of New Hampshire

What do you do?

I study how contaminants, such as oil and harmful chemicals, affect the environment and how microbes can break down the oil.

A lot of dispersants were used during the Gulf oil spill. What are they?

These chemicals help break up the oil into tiny droplets that get distributed into the water instead of floating on the surface.

What will the long-term effects of the spill be?

Only time will tell. More than a million gallons of dispersants have been sprayed on the water's surface or injected at the leak. We've never before come close to using that amount. We really don't understand what the impacts of doing that on a very large scale will be.

What's the greatest environmental concern with the Gulf oil spill?

When a spill occurs, you can't protect everything. That's why it is important to prioritize what needs to be done first. For this spill, everyone is working to save the wetlands and nearshore habitats. They are very important AND very hard to clean. On the other hand, areas like beaches are easier to clean. Workers can scoop up the contaminated sand and haul it away in trucks.

Controlled Burn

When an oil spill is very large, response crews need to take on more drastic measures to get rid of floating oil. For the Gulf spill, they performed controlled burns. Boats hauling fire-resistant boom dragged the oil to a remote area. Then it was set ablaze. The flames reached about 1,800°F (982°C). That's hot enough to melt steel. Some large fires burned as much as 48 barrels of crude oil in one minute.

Animals Under Threat

The Gulf of Mexico is a wildlife haven. More than 400 species of animals call the region home. The oil spill is not only threatening the animals' habitat, it's threatening their lives.

One reason oil is harmful to animals is because it depletes water of oxygen, the gas that animals breathe. Without oxygen, animals die. Some animals tried to escape from the oil slick. Dolphins and fish have been found clustered unusually close to the shore, far from their usual habitats at sea.

Bottlenose Dolphins

Every spring, up to 5,000 bottlenose dolphins calve, or give birth, in the shallow water in Breton Sound, near the Louisiana coast. Marine mammals, like dolphins, swim to the water surface for air. Breathing harmful gases given off by oil can irritate their lungs. It could lead to sicknesses like pneumonia.

Bluefin Tuna

These fish spawn, or lay their eggs, in the Gulf each spring. Females can lay as many as 10 million eggs a year. Since the eggs float in the water, oil can smother and kill them.

Shellfish

Shrimp and oysters, unlike fish, do not have fins. They're unable to swim away from the oil. The sludge could smother the shellfish and their babies, wiping out entire generations. Wildlife and humans are also at risk if they eat contaminated shellfish.

Sperm Whales

Like dolphins, these mammals need to surface to breathe. The chemicals in the oil can infect their skin and eyes.

Brown Pelicans

These birds dive beneath the water's surface to find food. If the seabirds eat fish tainted by the oil or feed it to their young, they can get sick or die. The oil can also destroy the birds' waterproof feathers. These feathers help seal the birds from freezing waters and also help them stay afloat. Damaged feathers mean that the birds could freeze to death or drown.

Sea Turtles

There are five sea turtle species that live in the Gulf of Mexico, of which four are endangered: Kemp's Ridley, leatherback, hawksbill, and green. The fifth species, the loggerhead, is threatened. The oil spill puts these turtles even more at risk of dying out.

Sea Turtle Expert

Name: Barbara Schroeder • Job: National Sea Turtle Coordinator at the National Marine Fisheries Service

What do you do?

My main focus is sea turtle recovery. I try to find ways to protect sea turtles from threats and help their populations grow.

Why are oil spills harmful to sea turtles?

If the animals eat oil or oiled-tainted fish, they could get stomach sicknesses. Worse, the oil could damage organs like livers or kidneys. This may kill the turtles.

How did you help during the Gulf oil spill?

We used planes to search for sea turtles and boats to rescue the ones caught in oily waters. We also examined dead turtles that washed ashore to figure out how exactly they died. In addition, we gave injured turtles medical attention.

How will this spill affect future generations of sea turtles?

It's a big threat to sea turtle populations. Turtles lay eggs on beaches. If the eggs are exposed to oil, they may not hatch. Young turtles that do hatch from the eggs may be born with damages. But that's not all. Turtles that were harmed by oil may have a hard time reproducing; they may not be able to lay eggs.

Animal Rescue Expert

Name: Tom MacKenzie • Job: Spokesperson for the U.S. Fish & Wildlife Service (USFWS)

What do you do?
I work for USFWS, a government agency that oversees wildlife protection. We have many scientists and volunteers working in the field. I work with the ones who operate in 10 southeastern states, Puerto Rico, and the Virgin Islands. I tell the public about their work.

How did the USFWS help to save the animals affected by the oil spill?
We helped set up decontamination sites and rehabilitation centers. We used booms to keep the oil away from the animals. We also responded to our hotline; it's like a 911 for wildlife. We received about 18 calls a day, telling us about injured birds or sea turtles. We searched for these animals. When we found them, we captured them and stabilized them by putting them in a crate. Then we took them to a rehabilitation center, where they would be evaluated and nursed back to health.

Rescue Squad
MacKenzie, holding a fishing net, and a colleague survey for injured wildlife.

Can nature help the cleanup process?
We noticed that it took the oil 50 days to travel 100 miles (160 kilometers) to reach the shores. During that time, the sun, tides, and wind helped evaporate benzene, a toxic chemical in the oil. This made the oil less dangerous to the wildlife. But still, any oil is bad.

How will this spill affect future generations of wildlife?
Scientists will be working for years to determine that. There are so many unknowns about this spill. Scientists will study, evaluate, and come up with lessons learned for future generations.

Wildlife Rescue

Wildlife experts worked quickly to rescue and clean up animals that had come in contact with the oil. One animal that holds a special significance to the Gulf is the brown pelican. This bird was officially named Louisiana's state bird in 1996.

Here's how the International Bird Rescue and Research Center rescues an oil-soaked pelican:

Operation Pelican

1. When an injured pelican is reported or discovered, bird experts race to the scene.

2. The experts transport the bird to a rehabilitation center in Buras, Louisiana. Immediately, the fragile, oil-soaked pelican is given medical attention.

3. When the bird is well enough, experts wash it by hand in a tub full of warm water with a dash of gentle-formula dishwashing liquid.

4. The pelican is rinsed with a high-pressure water nozzle. The number of bubble baths a pelican takes depends on its size and the amount of oil covering it. Once clean, the pelican sits under a pet grooming dryer.

5. A rehabilitated pelican gets released in eastern Florida, where it will not be recontaminated by the spill.

Stopping the Spill

One of the biggest challenges caused by the Gulf disaster was finding a way to stop the oil spill at its source. But that was no easy task. The gushing well, located 5,000 feet (1,500 meters) below sea level, is the deepest oil spill in history. Only remote-controlled robots can work at such depths. That's because humans can only dive up to 1,000 feet (300 meters) below sea level. Here are some methods BP used to try to control the spill.

Method 1: Repair It
Four robots were sent to the seafloor to repair the blowout preventer. The robots tried to activate the device, but it was completely broken.

Method 3: Squash It
As a last resort, BP drilled two relief wells. These wells snake thousands of feet into the rocky seabed. Their destination: the spot where the original well taps into the oil reservoir. Once there, the relief wells drill through the damaged pipe. Then they inject cement into the gusher to seal it off. This is the last resort because relief wells take months to complete.

Deepwater Horizon wreckage

Containment cap

Method 2: Cap It
As a temporary fix, BP covered the broken well with a containment cap. The cap sent the spewing oil up a tube connected to a tanker. This method helped collect several thousand barrels of oil per day. Unfortunately, what it could not collect continued to spill into the sea.

Relief well   **Relief well**

Oil Spill Expert

Name: Roger Anderson • Job: Oil geophysicist and professor of environmental science at Columbia University's Lamont-Doherty Earth Observatory

What do you do?

I study deepwater geology and drilling. I also study ways to drill relief wells when a blowout happens.

Why has it been so difficult to stop the Deepwater Horizon spill?

The oil is spilling from a well that is under more than a mile of seawater. We call areas like this the ultra-deepwater ocean. There, the seawater temperature is only 35°F (2°C) and the pressure is so high, it would crush most things. Under those conditions, we need to deal with gas hydrates. These ice crystals form when natural gas coming from the well meets the cold seawater and freezes.

Why do gas hydrates spell big trouble?

If you watch video footage of the spill, you'll see these ice crystals at work. They are what give the gushing oil that billowy look. These chunks of ice can clog the pipes of the caps that we send down below to try to control the oil spill. Basically, these crystals create plumbing problems. We need to pump down antifreeze to try to stop the ice from forming, but it is usually difficult to do so.

What will stop the oil from spilling?

The relief wells, I believe. That's what worked for the Ixtoc I oil spill in 1979. That was a very similar situation. It was in the Gulf of Mexico and it was an underwater blowout, too. Relief wells almost always work because they seal the leak at the source of the problem.

How will Deepwater Horizon change the way the world deals with future oil spills?

Many nations will launch huge research and development efforts. Countries like the U.S., Brazil, Gabon, Norway, Russia, China, and India all have huge oil reserves under ultra-deepwater. They will have to work on better blowout-prevention and disaster-response technologies to make sure such a terrible environmental disaster does not happen again.

For months after the Deepwater Horizon blowout, scientists and emergency response crews struggled to find ways to mop up the oil spill. Many people questioned: Are there newer and better ways to manage the oil slick? What can be done to prepare for future spills? Some innovative Americans have found some truly unusual ways to respond to oil disasters.

Super Water Filter

After seeing the damage caused by the *Exxon Valdez* oil spill in 1989, actor Kevin Costner felt moved to do something to fight oil spills. He invested more than $20 million of his own money into a company called Ocean Therapy Solutions. This company develops machines that can filter oil from polluted waters.

The machines work by sucking oily seawater into a centrifuge. This spinning contraption separates oil from the dirty water. The water, once cleaned, is returned to the ocean. The collected oil can be saved for usage. The largest model can filter polluted water at a rate of 200 gallons (757 liters) per minute, removing up to 99 percent of the oil from the water. After testing the machines and seeing promising results, BP placed an order.

Grease Mop

Hair, no matter if it's from humans or house pets, is a natural oil absorber. A nonprofit group called Matter of Trust collects snipped hair from salons around the country, using them to make special oil-absorbing mats and booms. In 2007, a tanker named *Cosco Buson* spilled oil into San Francisco Bay in California. Volunteers successfully used the hairy mats to help clean up greasy beaches.

Matter of Trust volunteers took it upon themselves to use hair mats and booms to soak up spilled oil from parts of the Gulf after the Deepwater Horizon disaster.

Experts of the Future

You're never too young to start making a difference. Meet two kid scientists.

Arthi Puri and Rani Iyer live in central Indiana. This area has many brownfields, or abandoned factories and commercial areas. These neglected properties are often contaminated with industrial waste or pollutants such as oil.

The two middle school students wanted to find a way to clean the land in their community. So they contacted Paul Schwab, a soil scientist at neighboring Purdue University, for advice.

Schwab explained how plants could be used to remove toxins from the ground. Arthi and Rani decided to test how well different types of plants could remove oil from tainted soil. Under Schwab's guidance, the girls gathered soil samples and got to work.

They found that one particular type of rye grass removed nearly half the oil from their soil samples in just six weeks! Arthi and Rani are now working with Schwab to set up a bigger project at a real brownfield.

Oil Eaters

Scientists have known for years that some bacteria and fungi chow down on oil. When oil is eaten, it is broken down into basic chemicals such as carbon dioxide, the gas you exhale. Luckily, there are already some of these creatures in the Gulf, but they won't be able to gobble up such a large amount of spilled oil.

Researchers are now studying these oil-eating creatures. They want to learn how the organisms break down oil. Scientists hope to use the information they uncover to create tools to remove future oil spills.

Think About It

Today, the world buzzes with technology like computers, TVs, and video games. They all need energy to power up, and much of that energy comes from oil. In the future, will other sources of energy take the place of oil?

Increasingly, Americans are turning toward renewable sources of energy, such as wind, water, and solar power. These types of energy naturally replenish much more quickly than nonrenewable resources like oil. Oil and other fossil fuels take millions of years to form.

Currently, renewable resources account for only 7 percent of our total energy supply. But breakthroughs in technologies that harness these types of energies may help to reduce our dependence on fossil fuels.

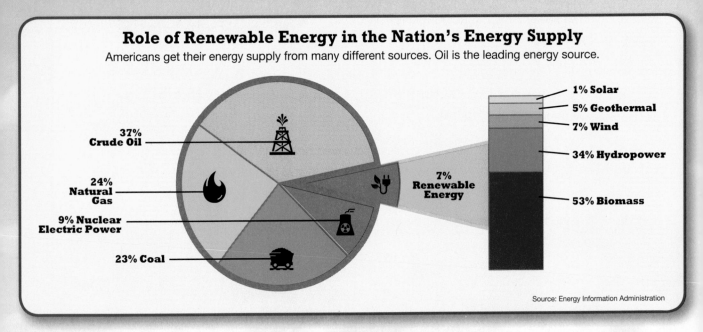

Role of Renewable Energy in the Nation's Energy Supply

Americans get their energy supply from many different sources. Oil is the leading energy source.

- 37% Crude Oil
- 24% Natural Gas
- 9% Nuclear Electric Power
- 23% Coal
- 7% Renewable Energy

- 1% Solar
- 5% Geothermal
- 7% Wind
- 34% Hydropower
- 53% Biomass

Source: Energy Information Administration

Oil and other forms of nonrenewable energy account for the largest percentage of our energy consumption. But even though replacing nonrenewable sources of energy with renewable ones may sound like a no-brainer, it's not that simple. There are benefits and drawbacks to every form of energy production.

Types of Renewable Energy

Wind

Giant structures called wind turbines turn the energy of moving air into electricity. Wind energy is clean because it does not emit any of the pollutants caused by burning fossil fuels. One problem with wind energy is that turbines are very easily damaged by storms. Also, wind energy is not as efficient as other methods and will never supply us with all of our energy needs.

Solar

Solar panels convert sunlight into electricity. Solar energy is one of the cleanest methods of energy production, but solar panels are very expensive to build. Some areas of the country might be better suited to solar energy than others. The Southwest, for example, is sunny most days of the year.

Geothermal

Geothermal energy production harnesses the heat energy from deep within the earth. Geothermal energy is regarded as very clean energy, but it is difficult, time-consuming, and costly to reach the energy hot spots beneath the earth.

Hydropower

Hydropower relies on dams to control the flow of water and convert the force of falling water into energy. This method is much more reliable than wind or solar power. Dams do not create pollution or waste, but they do change the ecosystem of the area, threatening animal habitats and plant life. Also, dams affect the quality of the water and cause soil erosion.

Biomass

Biomass comes from burning plant or animal waste. This type of energy helps reduce the amount of trash clogging up landfills. But the process to harness biomass is expensive. Fumes from burning the waste can also emit toxins into the environment.

As long as there is a need for oil, there will be risks associated with getting it, as we have seen in the Gulf. But what does the future look like? Will we continue to drill for oil under the sea? Will safer methods of extracting oil be invented? Or will new technologies allow us to harness renewable sources of energy more inexpensively and efficiently?

The answers to these questions will affect your future. You may even be the one who discovers a way to fulfill our energy needs without disasters like the one in the Gulf.

Glossary

Barrel: measurement for oil. One barrel equals 42 gallons.

Blowout: a sudden burst of gas or oil from a well

Dispersants: chemicals that break up an oil slick into tiny droplets

Ecosystem: a complex network of plants and animals that live within a community

Endangered species: type of plant or animal that is at risk of dying out

Erode: to wear away by wind or water

Flammable: easy to ignite or burn

Fossil fuel: fuel made from the remains of ancient plants and animals. Oil, coal, and natural gas are fossil fuels.

Geologist: scientist who studies the formation of Earth

Geophysicist: scientist who studies the physics of Earth and its atmosphere

National disaster: a declaration that allows resources from the federal government to be used in combating catastrophic events

Platform: massive structure that houses both the equipment and the workers necessary for drilling oil wells

Oil rig: a large platform used as a base for drilling for oil under the sea or underground

Plankton: tiny animals, plants, or bacteria that drift in water

Reserve: amount of crude oil estimated to be available

Threatened species: type of plant or animal that is at risk of becoming an endangered species

Wetlands: land where the soil is permanently or seasonally filled with moisture

Cleanup Crew
Two months after Deepwater Horizon exploded, its oil washed up on a beach in Alabama.